How to be an Amazing mother

6 best steps on how to be an astounding mother

by

Dr Smith Chapman

Copyright @2022 Dr Smith Chapman

TABLE OF CONTENTS

INTRODUCTION

A mother is the female parent of a child.

A woman may be considered a mother by virtue of having given birth, by raising a child who may or may not be her biological offspring, or by supplying her ovum for fertilisation in the case of gestational surrogacy. A mother is a person who carry 9 months in her belly, three years in her arms, and forever in her heart.

In this book, they are 6 common steps that can make you to be an amazing mother to your children's and also a valuable person in the family. Even if you're a working person the whole day that you don't have much time for her children, you will continue to be a mother whether you have one or more children, whether you're a working mother or stay at home mother,whether you live in a nuclear family or extended family. This book will help you to be the best mum you want to be for her little one's.

CHAPTER 1

Shouldn't feel down and out around night time when up with her young person.

In this part we will discuss these three things (the ought to, the shouldn't, the reliably). These three things is difficult for a mother to perceive while raising up her young people.

A. ☐ *The ought to:*

Help your kid's confidence: Once in a while it's not difficult to see when children appear to feel much better about them and when they don't we frequently depict having a decent outlook on ourselves as "confidence".

Messes around with confidence:

- Feel loved and acknowledged

- Feel certain

- Feel glad for what they can do

- Think beneficial things about themselves

Messes with low confidence:

- Are self-basic and tried on themselves

- Feel they're not on par with different children

- Consider the times they bomb instead of when they succeed

- Need certainty

- Question they can do things competently

B. ☐ *<u>The shouldn't:</u>*

It's normal for guardians to zero in on what they need to do to bring up solid children, however they frequently ignore what they ought not be doing.

The following are 10 things Guardians ought to NEVER Do

a.   Fail to administer them: There is the mind cerebrums which are associated with arranging, judgement, and drive control-are completely evolved until about age 25. In this manner, you want to go about as your kids' cerebrums until theirs create. This implies monitoring what your children are doing, with whom and assisting them with using sound judgement. This doesn't make you a parent who pays an excessive measure of regard for their kids rather, it shows the amount you give it a second thought.

Overall, it requires a long time from the investment a youngster start to develop symptoms of a psychological health condition to when they are seen for their most memorable psychiatric evaluation. Meanwhile, youngsters with untreated side effects of ADD/ADHD, uneasiness, wretchedness, bipolar disorder, or different issues can battle to prevail in school, in their kinships, and throughout everyday life.

c.   Do as I express, not as I do: Assuming you're an unfortunate good example, your children will get on that and take cues from you. For instance, assuming you say "eat your vegetables" however continually nibble on treats or potato chips, they will probably require the food they see you eating.

d.   Only notice what they foul up: Children just needs the consideration their folks, yet many possibly finish when they've something wrong, which builds up the negative ways of behaving. Rather than doing that, notice when your children do things you like-tidying up their room, completing their school work, or cleaning their teeth-and recognition them for their positive way of behaving.

e.   Be excessively lenient: Allowing your children to would anything that they like to make them "blissful" at the time, however it can hindering over the long haul. Youngsters need clear limits to assist them with understanding what isn't right. Do this by being firm however kind. Kids who have the most mental issues ordinarily have guardians who don't define limits for them.

f.   Be an unfortunate audience: When your children are attempting to converse with you, don't over them. Figure out how to be an attentive person. Allow them to get out whatever they need to and after ward talk back what you heard so they know your tuning in.

g.   Rarely invest quality energy with them: Solid parent-youngster connections call for exceptional time together. Quite possibly of the best thing you can do is spend somewhere around 20 minutes of value time every day with your time every day with your kid tuning in and doing something they believe that should do (sensibly speaking).

h.   Ignore the mind: Their cerebrum controls all that they do-how they think, and connect with others. At the point when their mind works right, they work right, however when their cerebrum is pained, they have inconvenience throughout everyday life. What's more, assuming that they have issues in their day to day existence, you have issues in yours.

i.   Use ridiculing: The greater part of guardians utilize a ruined name at whatever point their youngsters committed error, similar to "You're a ruined whelp" or say they are idiotic when they've committed an error or accomplished something wrong. This isn't useful for their turn of events. They will incorporate these negative names and start to accept them, which can unfavourably influence confidence.

j.   Ignore your own psychological wellness: Assuming you are experiencing any emotional well-being issues, it can obliterate your kids. Recollect the saving, "Put on your own breathing device first." You want to deal with yourself and be your best self so you can likewise be the best parent to them.

C. ☐ ***The reliably***:

Regardless of the kinds of discipline you use, it won't work in the event that you're not consistency is one of the more significant keys to tending to kid conduct issues.

Reliably setting limit, giving powerful outcomes and authorizing the principles all day regular can be intense, be that as it may. Look at what disrupts the general flow steady and do whatever it takes to build your discipline consistency.

Coming up next are steps on the best way to make your discipline reliable as a parent

a.   Pay thoughtfulness regarding your mind-sets

b.   Work with others guardians

c.   Expect change to take time

d.   Establish house rules

e.   Provide structure

f.   Develop an arrangement

g.   Choose your fights carefully

h.   Follow through with outcomes

i.   Resist to desire to surrender

j.   Focus on the long haul

CHAPTER 2

Talk about the Serious Stuff.

In particular, money and sex. "Normalizing sex is dire and holding on for a special day in what the future holds is putting the issue off endlessly," says David Ezell, an approved capable aide and Clinical Supervisor of Darien Well-being. So when exactly could it be prudent for you to bring this up? To be sure, sooner than you normally suspect. "Start when they are essentially nothing; long haul old will whine and be embarrassed while four years old will be responsive and open to anything you raise. Correspondingly as extensive as sex, cash is crucial for them to fathom starting from the start. Cash the board, spreading out goals with cash, sorting out cause — these are pressing major capacities that ought to be kept an eye on immediately."

I accept any sensible individual would concur that every single one of us enters life as a parent with a lot of convictions or suspicions in regards to being a nice mother. We cultivate these convictions from the strain of our organizations and society all things considered, the experiences with our own people, and through the suppositions for sidekicks, family, and media. These outside effects can have such a ton of power and effect over us that when we finally become mothers ourselves, it is excruciatingly difficult to focus on our own considerations of what this "extraordinary mother" thing is about.

So irksome, truly, that anxiety, awfulness, and overwhelming tendency can snare on like crazy to our new person.

I really want to give a brief tale to you a tracked down in my about a mother office this pre-summer. This mother has permitted me to share her cycle around the subject of being a fair mother, since it gives such an undeniable outline of the way stickler thinking and impossible presumptions can provoke torment.

CHAPTER 3

Always does what is best for her child

A decent mother makes a huge difference and the significance of mom's can't be put into words. A mother assumes many parts throughout her youngster's life - every one crucial to forming her kid in various ways. Whether she is the essential guardian, working guardian, or both she holds an extraordinarily significant job in her loved ones.

A mother is a first educator of each and every youngster during youth. The synaptic organizations in a youngster's mind are as yet being shaped during the initial five years of their lives. Youngsters at this stage are especially open to human contact. How guardians connect with their kids and draw in them in mental, social and close to home formative exercises during these years will characterize their future selves. A mother can be in touch with her kid's educator to remain refreshed what the youngster realizes in the study hall and assist with supporting and move this learning in the home setting.

A mother job helps in changing a kid from pre-school to kindergarten. Change is when mom's can have significant associations with their kids. Clarify for your youngster what will occur previously, during and after the progress. Preparing, creating required abilities and involving changes as conversational pieces will assist with diminishing the general pressure of your kid. Mom's are urged to give additional warmth like embraces and consoling words. Making yourself accessible to help your youngster can likewise give him/her heaps of confirmation.

The following are five things that will make a mother best for her kids

I.   Be a decent good example.

II.   Love your kid and show them love through activities, like embraces, investing energy with them and paying attention to them.

III.   Be a place of refuge. Youngsters raised by guardians who answer reliably will have a superior social and close to home turn of events.

IV.   Talk with your youngster, as this assists their mind with incorporating. At the point when various pieces of the mind are incorporated, they capability amicably and prompts more co-usable way of behaving and more sympathy.

V.   Pay regard for your own prosperity. Take great consideration of yourself genuinely, sincerely and intellectually. Find opportunity to reinforce your relationship with your life partner. Assuming that these regions fall flat, your kid will endure as well.

CHAPTER 4

Always puts youngster's necessities before her own

Putting your kids needs first will assist with safeguarding your physical and mental life span for those you care about most. Guardians ought to be more mindful of how they feel and where they feel it.

Constantly, when a mother finds she can't necessarily do everything, the one region she won't let slide is her obligation to her youngsters. She'll forego purchasing another satchel assuming that it implies her child can have the top brand of soccer spikes. She will surrender a get-together with a dear companion to hurry to school with a kid's failed to remember task.

While such a mentality is estimable, there are times when a mother gives her youngsters a raw deal by answering their every beck and call. Now and again, putting her own n

CHAPTER 5

Teach her adolescent the meaning of confidence:

Kids who feel quite a bit better about themselves have the certainty to attempt new things. They are bound to make an honest effort. They feel pleased with what they can do. Confidence assists jokes around with adapting to botches. It assists jokes around with attempting once more, regardless of whether they fall flat from the beginning. Subsequently, confidence assists jokes around with improving at school, at home, and with companions.

Jokes with low confidence feel uncertain of themselves. On the off chance that they figure others will not acknowledge them, they may not participate. They might allow others to mistreat them. They might struggle with supporting themselves. They might surrender effectively, or not attempt by any means. Jokes with low confidence find it hard to adapt when they commit an error, lose, or fall flat. Thus, they may not work out quite as well as they could.

How Confidence Creates

Confidence can begin as soon as childhood. It grows gradually after some time. It can begin in light of the fact that a kid has a solid sense of reassurance, cherished, and acknowledged. It can begin when a child stands out and cherishing care.

As infants become babies and small kids, they're ready to do a few things without anyone else. They feel better about themselves when they can utilize their new abilities. Their confidence develops when guardians focus, let a kid attempt, give grins, and show they're glad.

As children develop, confidence can develop as well. Any time kids attempt things, get things done, and learn things can be an opportunity for confidence to develop. This can happen when kids:

- gain ground toward an objective

- learn things at school

- make companions and get along

- acquire abilities — music, sports, craftsmanship, cooking, techs abilities

- Practice most loved exercises

- help, give, or be thoughtful

- get acclaim for good ways of behaving

- make a solid attempt at something

- do things they're great at and appreciate

- are incorporated by others

- feel got it and acknowledged

- get an award or a passing mark they realize they've procured

At the point when children have confidence, they feel certain, able, and acknowledged for what their identity is.

How Guardians Can Fabricate Confidence

Each youngster is unique. Confidence might come simpler to certain children than others. Furthermore, a few children face things that can bring down their confidence. Yet, regardless of whether a kid's confidence is low, it very well may be raised.

Here are things guardians can do to assist messes around with having a decent outlook on themselves:

Assist your kid with figuring out how to get things done. At each age, there are new things for youngsters to learn. In any event, during childhood, figuring out how to hold a cup or make first strides ignites a feeling of dominance and joy. As your youngster develops, things like figuring out how to dress, read, or ride a bicycle are opportunities for confidence to develop.

While showing kids how to get things done, show and help them from the start. Then let them give their very best, regardless of whether they commit errors. Be certain your kid has an opportunity to learn, attempt, and feel pleased. Try not to make new difficulties excessively simple — or excessively hard.

Acclaim your youngster, yet do it astutely. Obviously, lauding kids is great. Your commendation is a method for showing that you're glad. Be that as it may, a few different ways of commending children can really misfire.

This is the way to get everything done as well as possible:

• Try not to over praise. Acclaim that doesn't feel acquired doesn't sound accurate. For instance, telling a youngster he played an incredible game when he realizes he didn't feels empty and phony. It's smarter to say, "I realize that wasn't your best game, yet we as a whole have off days. I'm pleased with you for not surrendering."

Add a demonstration of positive support: "Tomorrow, you'll be back on your game."

•   Acclaim exertion. Try not to zero in acclaim just on results, (for example, getting A) or fixed characteristics, (for example, being savoy or athletic).

All things being equal, offer a large portion of your commendation for exertion, progress, and demeanour. For instance: "You're really buckling down on that venture," "You're getting endlessly better at these spelling tests," or, "I'm glad for you for rehearsing piano — you've truly stayed with it." With this sort of acclaim, kids put exertion into things, make progress toward objectives, and attempt. At the point when that's what children do, they're bound to succeed.

Be a decent good example. At the point when you put exertion into regular errands (like raking the leaves, making a dinner, tidying up the dishes, or washing the vehicle), you're setting a genuine model. Your youngster figures out how to invest energy into doing school work, tidying up toys, or making the bed.

Displaying the right demeanour counts as well. At the point when you take care of assignments merrily (or if nothing else without protesting or grumbling), you help your kid to do likewise. At the point when you try not to race through tasks and invest wholeheartedly in nicely done, you help your kid to do that as well.

Boycott brutal analysis. The messages kids catch wind of themselves from others effectively converts into how they feel about themselves. Unforgiving words ("No doubt about it!") are hurtful, not inspiring. At the point when children hear negative messages about themselves, it hurts their confidence. Right children with tolerance. Centre around what you believe they should do sometime later. When required, show them how.

Centre on qualities. Focus on what your youngster gets along nicely and appreciates. Ensure your youngster has opportunities to foster these qualities. Centre more around qualities than shortcomings if you have any desire to assist messes with having a decent outlook on them. This further develops conduct as well.

Allow children to help and give. Confidence develops when children get to see that what they do matters to other people. Children can assist at home, do a help project at school, or help out for a kin. Aiding and kind demonstrations assemble confidence and other positive

sentiments

CHAPTER 6

Provide food, safe house, and love

As a parent or guardian, you assume a significant part in moulding your kids' dietary patterns. You have a major impact over the family climate where dinners occur and the sorts of food sources your kids eat. Positive encounters about food right off the bat might assist your youngsters with creating good dieting propensities further down the road. Peruse on to figure out how to decidedly impact your youngsters' dietary patterns by establishing a positive eating climate and being a decent good example.

Establishing a positive eating climate

Family dinners happen in the home (or the "eating climate"). This eating climate can assist with making a positive effect on your kids' dietary patterns. The following are a couple of tips to assist you with establishing a positive eating climate for your kids.

i. Have ordinary dinner and titbit times

Having normal feast and bite times regular makes a solid daily schedule. Assuming youngsters nibble just before feasts or top off on drinks like milk or plant-based refreshments, they may not be ravenous when now is the right time to eat, which can affect the food sources they decide to eat at supper time. Plan to offer a dinner or nibble each 2 to 3 hours during the day. In the event that your youngster says they are eager before the booked feast or titbit, offer nutritious food sources like cut up veggies or natural product.

ii.   Eat all together

Youngsters who eat dinners with their family will generally eat better food varieties like natural products, vegetables and entire grains. They are likewise bound to keep a solid body weight. The significance of family dinners goes past nourishment. Research shows that eating dinners with relatives additionally has numerous different advantages like expanded jargon in small kids and diminished risk for substance maltreatment in youngsters. It very well might be challenging to design family feasts with occupied plans - begin by arranging a couple of family dinners during the week when you are less occupied, as on ends of the week.

Attempt themed feasts to get your children amped up for coming to the supper table. A few plans to attempt:

•	Cook out style dinner - offer an assortment of finger food sources like veggies, natural product, entire grain wafers, cheddar, nuts and seeds. Lay a sweeping in the lounge to partake in the dinner together.

•	Make your own Silly Face Pizza night

•	Variety topic evenings - like "green" night where you serve just green food varieties. Attempt these Green Meatballs served with Pea Shoot Pesto Pasta and Ground Up Frog Smoothies

iii.	Try not to compel your youngsters to eat

Demanding that your youngsters eat specific food varieties may really make them eat less. Allow your kids to choose the amount to eat at feasts and bites in light of how hungry they feel. Are eating times a battle? Express farewell to demanding eating with these tips.

Try not to involve food as a prize or discipline

Involving food as a prize or discipline might prompt undesirable dietary patterns. Offer different nutritious food varieties at dinner and titbit times and let your kids serve themselves with no tension. Make an effort not to name food sources as "great" or "terrible" or "sound" and "undesirable."

iv. Have good food varieties at home

The food varieties accessible in your refrigerator, cooler, cabinets and storeroom are what your kids will become accustomed to eating. Utilize this menu arranging structure to assist you with arranging nutritious dinners as a family!

v. Being a positive good example

Guardians can impact their kids' dietary patterns in a positive manner by being a decent good example. Here are a few hints on the most proficient method to be a decent good example with regards to food.

Go with quality food sources the standard decision

What you eat sets a model for what your kids will eat. Appreciate food sources from Canada's Food Guide consistently, for example, vegetables, organic product, entire grain items and protein food sources like beans, nuts and seeds, tofu, eggs, fish, lean meats, yoghurt and milk. At the point when your kids see you eating these food varieties, they are bound to need to eat them as well.

Limit food sources high in calories, fat, sugar and salt

While purchasing bundled food sources look at names and pick food sources lower in immersed fat, sugar and salt. Look at this article for tips on name perusing.

Have a go at making prepared products and snacks yourself. At the point when you set up your own, you can lessen how much sugar, immersed fat and salt utilized. Make a major bunch and freeze divides independently for a speedy expansion to school snacks or for an after school nibble. Attempt these Radiant Energy Chomps, Granola and Natural product Nibbles or Flying Saucer Biscuits.

Attempt a portion of these youngster accommodating recipes:

Yoghurt Granola Mountain

Apple Cinnamon Heated Oats

Smaller than expected Meatballs

Mango Dark Bean Salad

Sweet and Crunchy Carrot Salad

What might a dietician do?

A dietician will assist with ensuring your youngster is getting significant supplements like protein, fibre, iron and calcium that your kid needs to develop and be

9 798351 991771